NATURAL VIOLENCE

NATURAL VIOLENCE

Jennifer Brown

BRICK ROAD
POETRY PRESS

Brick Road Poetry Press
www.brickroadpoetrypress.com

Library of Congress Number: 2022938766
ISBN: 978-1-950739-07-3

Published by Brick Road Poetry Press
341 Lee Road 553
Phenix City, AL 36867
www.brickroadpoetrypress.com

Brick Road logo by Dwight New

To B., my favorite

Table of Contents

I. Vocabulary & Exercises

II. Composition & Rehearsal

III. Recitations & Incantations

I. Vocabulary & Exercises

Villanelle for the Real World with a Line from Voltaire

Remember that all the known world is governed by books,
said Voltaire. The unknown, too, like the wastes
beyond your gates, takes shape as you look

up from the page. That dead land, darkened by rooks,
seethes with meaning, now that your mind has raced
to remember all the known world. Governed by books,

you're prone to gaze out the window as the talk crooks
its way round the room. Your mind, like a horse, makes haste
beyond the gates, takes shape as you. Look,

you can barely tell who you are until time hooks
your flesh. The mind, always flying, is braced
to remember. All the known world is governed. By books

we are stolen away, set trembling, shook,
dispatched to borderless regions none has traced.
Beyond, the gates take shape. As you look,

the wild overtakes the known. This is all it took
to claim you once, child by wild embraced.
Remember that. All the known world's governed by books.
Beyond the gates, desire takes shape. You look.

Primary School

The hardening runnels of sap I pressed my fingers in
as a child—only a child looks at pines so closely,
the way she watches the clear sap
leak from her scraped shin after blood stops
& wonders if this is how she will leave her body,
this little by little.

The child learns the words to songs—sings
untuned before sleep. Her brother chants
& rocks & falls asleep, sheet-wrapped & hot.
She likes to sing & feel her throat clench—
If you miss the train I'm on, you will know that I have gone...
She lies awake.

Once upon a time, words brought her sorrow—

Pyrite & Mica

For my brother

Summers, we camped near gem shows
booked in cheap hotels—blue or black velveted
tables of agate chessboards, *malachite* in trays,
an *onyx* menagerie we coveted. By an emptied mine,
crystals sharp as the name our father gave us

to call them: *pyrite*, two confident syllables,
mastery over those winking dice—a fortune
in foundering hope, common name: *fool's gold*.
A pretty fantasy, until a test of hardness
& weight: then, brilliance had to be enough,

true metal untwinned from its image—
what could be enough to satisfy? We wanted
pockets full to rub our fingers on, to hold
all the way home in the new light of the words
we'd learned—*aventurine. Rhodochrosite.*

Rutilated quartz. The facts: *snowflake obsidian*
is volcanic glass. *Semi-precious.* We scuffed
around the empty hard clay lot next door,
unearthing rocks & bursting them,
thinking *iron makes the clay this rusted red.*

There, *limestone* lay in dull beads: shell & bone.
Sometimes, a chunk of *quartz*, dirt-white like teeth,
or, silvered opaque, a slab of *mica*, or *granite*
sequined with it. Fooled—we'd flake its layers,
watch it drift & cling to us like fish-scales,

11

peel papery, doll-sized windowpanes
to hold to our eyes, grayed monocles.
Poor transparency, call it *isinglass*, or *shelter*,
or *portal*, let its pigment be tint against glare
& dismantle mirages rising on the hot street.

Let it turn solid. Mineral. Its sudden beauty,
fraying crumbled edges. We'd gather
what we'd need to build small cities,
twinned, separate: selves we hadn't given
to words. Mica could double as glass & shone

like silver. What didn't fail us? Brilliance lasted
as long as light was a single thing touching down,
was rough & silvered in our hands,
let them make what they could, let them grow
strange to each other as each cell'd repeat itself,

double helices doubling & wrenched apart,
the membranes translucent, permeable, distinct,
defining. Replication. Division.
What we are now, we were then. We wanted
to rescue each other, builders of forms.

We knew *the saw that cut rock would not cut skin.*
But there were some names we'd never know, dark
shapes that rose in the dark of our eyes
in sleep. *Solder* & *flux.* In time, even
trees would turn to stone, what we trusted.

Beginning Geography

In another room, parents' voices.
Syllables crowd & steamroll one another,
the murmur like distant construction
or demolition, edifice or vacant lot.

On the page before me, a list
of capital cities, lakes & rivers,
birds & flowers. Maps in pastel colors.
All the wonder of the world translated,

packed for my daily travels. The book,
with its fragrance of tedious wisdom,
lies open & shut at once. Open or
shut, the door to this room, as to each

room in the house, is barricade & freeway.
Inside & outside are its subjects.
Inside & outside, the citizens
claim what they can for themselves.

Into the Woods

Under a tarp strung clear across dewy,
heavy air, we sleep communal
on crackling plastic in the dark acres
behind the lake. There is singing

by guitar & spider-hunt by flashlight
held to the forehead, a way to leave
the fire & hold hands with someone
a few charged moments. Then back,

no secrets showing. We think it's chance
the way the cabins are paired, this boys'
with that girls', not the counselors' design,
who together sleep by the fire, away

from their charges. In the first quiet
of lying down, some girl tells the story:
entire camping groups missing in the woods,
or maybe one girl at a time, maybe only

those who strayed alone too far into the trees.
The last ones to fall asleep hear a carnival
of sound, amplified with every cracking twig,
every rhythm that must, we fear, be footfalls.

Daddy-Long-Legs tickles us like night's fingers.
Soon, someone wakes with a kick, sits up, touched
on her face or hair. We're 12, 13, 14.
We hear something's there before we can name it.

Badlands & Canyon

From old Route 66 in Arizona,
neon diners release us to this:
Triassic floodplain, desert basin. Rock
trees litter these bitten dunes; under them

sleep stone dragons. Roped-off rooms of a pueblo
in ruins are backdrops for family
photos—*Smile!* Once, we read, a swollen river
tore trees from roots, washed them north to strange land,

scoured ripe earth clean & painted it iron
& manganese, reds, yellows, indigos,
black, carbon-gray. On vertical faces,
glyphs of a language we cannot decode—

still, we argue over meanings as if
rightness won loyalty, as if knowing
were a trophy. Archaeology loves
its trowels & calipers, its screens,

augurs, & scales. Spruce & palm, an agate
forest lies cracked to the sun like fruit,
Aladdin's jewel-garden at my feet.
If I fill my hands & pockets, am I

a thief or lover? At an overlook,
my brother beside me, my mother
& father, so small—I can almost reach
them, each alone in a desert, descending

between canyon walls, finding river's green,
its chanted story dreamlike & rife.
This is birth—each of us into silence
that locks the canyon to a sky distant,

flecked with hawks. We climb bald, shifting dunes,
shadows like ciphers spelling ourselves

to ourselves in the ruins before us.

Memory Is a Body Concealed

This is the way the clouds filled in the valleys—

soft humps of mountain surfacing
like a long-believed-in Loch Ness monster's spine.
We thought we'd been driving on mainland

& were moored, but here were only beachheads,

as far as we could see, islands connected
by a body—concealed—below us.
It was a place we'd never been, the hush of water

gathering up as rain, water making itself

a white sea in the air. The sky was still sky.
We clicked pictures with simple cameras to prove
we'd been there truly, that it was no Olympus

of our minds' eyes—

white & blue & separate from us
by a veil of mist we felt on our skin.
It was not dreamed, though we would wish our dreams

were that full of the stilled shapes of waves

& a sense of having risen
from a worn network of roads to a sky
that laps at our feet like ocean.

Our pictures would be small, dim squares

that hinted at what we'd seen, darkening
from the edges as if to admonish us that a moment
is only ever ungraspable.

But I can phone my brother, hold his voice to my ear—

so like my own, the roar of sea in a shell—say
Do you remember when the cliffs on either side of us
gave way to a cloud-Atlantic dreaming of its old bed,

to a brief & unfathomable Pacific?

Gulf

Dawn fog, thunderheads, cold front coming in,
wind from the plains, weather that weathers us—
we *whether*. Rain curtains. Blinds we cannot open.
The sea swells toward the heartland: *kolpos,*
Greek for bosom—it enfolds, is the seat
of rhythm, will not becalm. Whether *we*
are or not, it buoys, it ebbs, it is warm there
to plunge into. Another front shreds us here
& here, wrecks of weather—mercy what we find
or make in the flood's path, what washes fair
on our shore, beached, irrevocable, exposed.
Refuse. The dead. The broken-beyond-repair.
We've weathered. Litter tossed on this
hard shore: storm-salvage, love, worn gift.

Unreconciling

Then the storm stripped bark from the sycamore,
laid loosening scrolls on the ground, the trunks
holding silvered limbs up bare in hot rain.
"Like nymphs," I said, "like the rain undressed them."

He looked at the trees. "No, they're not," he said.
Later I said, "Here fireflies will rise
from earth at twilight like heroes pinning
history in the sky." He shook his head.

"No," he said, looking out across the slow
Susquehanna, islands gray-green in haze.
"Like Avalons," I said, "like some sphinx
risen from the river, our quest unveiled."

He walked to the guardrail. "No," he said.
"There's water. There's earth. Here's a bench
of concrete & pine. We are all alone
out here," he said. The river flashed

its many eyes, roiling. "Hush," I said. *Don't
listen*, I whispered to the water, gently
as I could. "People will think you're crazy,"
he said, "talking to the empty air like that."

Never Hurt Me

Words must be weighed
like metals & gems, tapped
& drilled, x-rayed,
bitten with a skeptic's tooth,
arraigned for betrayal, severed
from their families,
exhausted. Disarmed.
Like air travelers, they're suspect
without sheaves of documents.
They might secret a bomb,
hide a shiv, their costumes
so common, their companions
the same, impeccable.
They overrun, spill from screens,
mouths, rooms, speakers.

Words are gathering
right here, arrayed
with opaque smiles, neat
parcels of—what?
Squint at them, they'll squint back.
What will you do about them?
You want to trust them.
They impress you, mark you.
When they leave, exhaled
from the darkness, what
will they carry away?

II. Composition & Rehearsal

Circadian

Tonight, again, sleep. As in a hushed tank
I'd float weightless, unseeing, detached from
solid forms. Still, but traveling. Self-built,

this maze, its features redrawn anew each
go-round. The body plunges out of need,
craving blackout, a wordless feast alone.

Tonight, again, rehearsal. This is how
to weather *alone*. She braves the dead
of sleep who drifts as if lost by gravity's

arms, her hair the texture of night. It's not
a tourist's untrammeled passage, drive-by
faces glancing along shined surfaces,

mute mysteries unplumbed. Tonight, again,
I drag for something to wrest from the depth
& carry to day, something to transform.

Again, I'll sink in sleep as into death
& hold a line to emerge by. Morning
spills across my newly rewritten face.

Greeting a Neighbor in the First Hour of Light

Early morning insists. Each leaf,
branch, & stem is edged in fine white,
veins like fretwork. Sun brings up color.
Each breath hangs briefly as cloud,

footprints lodge green in gray grass,
& a word spoken to hail a stranger
surprises the tongue in its lassitude,
surprises by its form, its clear unlikeness

to undisturbed air. It resembles
the first miraculous intelligence
of a mute from the far province within,
the words themselves helpless to say

whether they will be unlatched like gifts
or will fall to the cold earth unheard.
How does the mute draw these vessels
from the well in the desert, the mine

in which she unearths the mineral
self? There is the ore of the known.
It reaches the surface as words, crystalline,
striated, loosed from slag & shining.

The Russian word for *old* sounds like *starry*,
& each describes that reference book
to which we've always looked: the starry night,
English or Russian, is older than memory.

In the risen light, only Venus remains shining.
We keep the old map buried in our darkness.
Cracked open, words release
what we've always known, pass it on beyond us.

Until Daylight & the Train

Rats behind motel paneling give lessons in how
not to sleep in the Big Easy, chewing the edges
of a 12-hour layover, the solid ground between trains
that sweep the lower south from Houston
to Washington, but not so smoothly as the verb
to sweep implies; no, the iron horses move
like horses, stopping to graze sometimes,
or like my sleep here, in a motel
"near the business district & French Quarter"
(said the travel agent, who had never seen it),
down a four-lane stretch of New Orleans highway,
down from the train station, a short cab ride,
open windows pulling in streams of damp June air—

like my sleep here, in the LONDON LODGE
of the unlit, peeling sign, of consumptive septuagenarian
manning the check-in with crabbed yellow hands,
ignoring the door buzzer for the flash of TV
blueing his gray face, in the Lodge of such Obvious Decline
that the cabbie says "whatchya stayin here for
girl?" & rips me off for double the fare—

like my sleeping here, the trains' sweeping isn't sweeping
at all, but a rough, interrupted trundle through
time, trying to be seamless, trying to avoid
delays, interference, accidents—& here, someone's hair
on the sheets, rotary telephone, broken air conditioner,
an inch space between door & doorframe, rickety lock—

here (I have just told the one I once loved
that we are through), the television tuned

by previous occupant to local-feed porn, "Four Play Video,"
the rats chewing & chewing their way in
as if to keep me fearful, to keep me from rest,
from shutting out booming music, cars revving,
harangues exchanged in the hall,
the disorder & mess, the foreign, the ugly,
the coded & impenetrable landscape
where I fear the rats will find me on top of the still-made bed,
TV on, the 39-year-old, pot-bellied, pony-tailed,
balding man in his trademark (he says) socks
demonstrating "doing it doggie"—

here, no clock, no wake-up call, no bathtub,
moldy shower, lying on flea market furniture,
I watch this staged fucking until
daylight & the train arrive like a single sweet chariot
that will not, of course, carry me home at all,
but only to the next temporary stop: gnawed sleep,
irretrievable lies, my single sentence.

Natural Violence

Her mother's hypodermic words, the tracks they left.
Her mother's silent mouthfuls of crushed ice.
His father pinned his arms. *Just wrestling*, he said.
Lover who threatens to leave but comes back & stays.

It's no use, but try not repeating this.
Ever the turn & the turn against.

Spring is back, & the rain, & then all's clear.
Fiddleheads skewer debris, stems spear soil,
birds chisel out of shells. How many things
we break, trying to live. What, in this world

can hold or hold us? Here is the turn, a nest
blown down, all needles of grass, air & angles.
A cup the shape of its maker's flown breast.
It cannot be returned to. It cannot be mended.

A Big Easy Sestina

Visiting the coast of the Gulf—it is humid,
this I knew once & have kept, a dull
story I sometimes tell about a lost quarter
of my life. You know how the past, like a train
through town mid-afternoon, misguided
despite its tracks, stops traffic, shears the undivided

muddle into a neat impasse, each onlooker's undivided
attention face-forward, for once, squinting & humid
& waiting to be released to motion. I miss, guided
by longing, what's just ahead, until, dulled
by my own lazy wit, I train
my eyes on the hands I've quartered

before me. But they are not my own. I've given time no quarter,
but it has settled here anyway. I am one, divided
in the usual ways, like the last camper waiting for the train,
already feeling the knife of loss & the humid
breath of home, that sleeping bear. *Now* is often dull—
as Joseph Brodsky said, *boring*: misguided

well-intentioned work & talk, misguided
understandings & alliances. Even in the French Quarter,
where good times are said to roll, *now* is dulled
& choked by memory as a pond by plants, an undivided
green fog that kills the fish. Humid,
breezy, this city looks to the untrained

like any other: shiny, peopled, crumbling, the train
clattering in sloppy time to the stories we, misguided,
keep on telling. We stand by what we were. *Only human,*
I tell myself. Like an old-time traitor drawn & quartered,
I destroy myself, past & present divided
until I see you, out of time & place, my tongue dull

but laden, as if before my gift of bones, the idol
had roared my name. So long ago, you left by train
& I remained in that town, my grief undivided,
pure. Then dimming, then gone. Yet we didn't miss, guided
by nothing, this rendezvous, here, in the storied quarter
of sin & song. What survives time? A humid

ill-kept love jumps the train, runs unguided
through humid alleys. But its old quarters,
much-divided, are gone. Loss thrums dull in my throat.

Retraction

When she woke up near him, when
she was leaving & he rested his forehead on hers
& stayed that way for a moment,
she believed.

Later, when he turned his face to her
& said some words, it felt
as if a boy had suddenly laughed
& dashed a handful of sand in her face,
although it looked as though he simply shut a door,
on which appeared a new face, identical
to the first, but with a closed door behind it.

Consignment

Dressed to strangle, like Frankenstein's monster:
my new second-hand skin donated
by the fashionable or the dead, their closets
sorted through by daughters & neighbors—
I could be ready to go anywhere

in this satiny, slightly pilled scarlet sweater,
in the skirt a size small but the perfect hue,
tight in that starlet way across the hips—don't look
too close & it's glamorous—these shoes
already slant-worn at the heels, tipping my gait unsteady.

I could've been ready to see you, with your—yes—
salesman's smile & doe-eyes, your mime's hands insisting
a world one almost believes is there,
your mechanic's hands failing at reconstruction,
that pull & pick at your shirt patched

on the heartside with someone else's name.
I am a miserable seamstress, too impatient—
my alterations always look like compromise, uneasy
truce drawn between me & my materials. You
had that half-sewn look, you seemed too much—

& I, shear-tongued, needle-eyed:
don't be fooled. I'm not got up as smart
as I think. Tonight, shepherding someone else's house
& pets, I'm the little girl in the corner, quiet,
moving letters around a puzzle: hope—open,

heart—tart—art—useless to redress harm.
Or maybe not. Say it: these thrift-shop clothes
crease with my body like my own skin.
You're back with her. I have here your efficient,
dishwasher's hands, guiltless, bleached

exceptionally clean, your eyes-in-absentia,
little targets——. Anger is too much work.
On someone else's TV, I watch Koko,
the signing gorilla, name a tailless kitten "All-Ball,"
scoop the splay-footed mewing thing

onto her chest, gentle-handed. Someone else's dog
lays his head on my leg. Can it hurt to love
someone else's dog? It's when All-Ball dies
& Koko signs "frown-sad-cry"
that I weep, safe in a room where nothing is mine.

Light Is Not the Only Constant

At nearly winter solstice, the light falls
differently than when you began to live
here, in this room, this too-simple box
to contain you. Now the angles
of evening are sharp & brief. Morning's cold
hands intrude on long sleep. Tight as it is,
the room has held you—nutshell of infinite
space, launch-pad. Bed. Closet. Clock. Mirror.
By harnessed light, you regard your image
warmly, by thin day, spot the net of hair-fine
veins beneath the skin. All light lost, you
disappear, eyes extinguished, mirror black.
But you are still here. Hand to face confirms,
the inward eye sees truly. You are you.

Refusing to See Saltcedars as Weeds

In the fallow West of Texas, you
roll through ghost-towns where metal signs creak
in the windy aftermath of RV
traffic, where houses unpeopled might lift

on tall wheels & roll themselves to the Alamo,
New Orleans, LA to NYC in 19 days.
Their roofs threadbare, each a rictus blank-eyeing
buzzards circling on thermals. Everything wants to roll.

Houses lie open to the sky as though their hearts
had been torn out in some kind of rapture, swollen so
with the sight of yucca candling at dusk, the miles
growing inside their walls, summers of drought,

limestone hills, rock fallen, cracked to gravel,
gravel to sand, sand to dust. You think of reduction,
breakdown, evisceration, how all things tend
this way, these Death's mile markers, farther

& farther apart. You see the river, hidden
by its own knifing in a V of rock, cold at the end
of a hot hike down, feathery salt-cedars overarching
desertwillow, lowering the water-table.

The river bends in & out of sight, green thread
fraying into streams & washes, dividing itself
endlessly, you think, as long as anything
can sew its roots into rock & find the end

of dessication there. Dust & light—a ripe seed
drifts down grave air to the bathed banks,
the way the memory of a sight settles deep
inside you, drinking up what releases root & bud.

Railway

Along Amtrak's Southern Crescent, tin-roofed houses,
industrial storage, factories, rust-riveted machines
that whine to life tomorrow for the aching work-week.

Green-grey clouds piling tropical towards the start
of summer's violences, the flood drains gurgle & ditches
stagnate in the chemical-green bloom of algae.

In noon sun, a group of darkening boys,
bikes at the ready by the tracks, gesture at us
who are framed in the windows of the trundling

metal intrusion, themselves framed long enough
that I watch each boy's threshing blur of skinny arms,
feet & hands the size of men's almost,

palms hardening in dimes at each finger's base.
The scene changes too quickly to see
if they mean to cheer us on or to protest us.

The group's united only by the eye's making a picture
out of separate pools of light, transcribing
road & crossroad, the parallel footpath,

the flat, rigid ladder of track overlying swamp
& open water, liquid floored forests, tea-dark.
Stolen topsoil lines the reticent bayous,

the Atchafalaya basin speaks in shifting Atlantises,
temporary, unmappable, dividing the waters.
Those long phrases of streams & channels

emerge & recede as the train passes,
their plots abandoned in the low branches dying
under garlands of Spanish moss & what

those ragged lines refuse. Waters
only navigable by ones or twos in motorless skiffs
who find the way by nerve & fickle light,

by disbelief in the finality of being lost:
wakes smoothing out to catch the leaves
describe the departure of some undaunted naturalist

who took the long, slow way inside,
the way that turns & is overgrown, that opens
like stadia & closes like coffins overhead,

that shows, sometimes, to the patient eye,

a single, shy, disappearing species of wader
probing for food at knotty roots in its chapel
of just enough light to see by.

From the train, I see the trees tilt & crowd,
scoured & splintered like gravestones,
the wakes subside & branches knit across the heart

of this wetland whose waters rise & rush
to consume us rushing away on the tracks,
elevated, efficient, longing——. & I see, too,

these expanses where the deep swamp
opens to summer's offices, fields lush
to the horizon, the baking scent of damp earth

alive on my tongue. Against the green
& dimming sky, like desire hunting,
cattle egrets lift & plunge.

Spectacle

Back in the woods after a week's steady rain,
I look for what newly pushes up
through the mulch of deep leaves, bark,
& whatever else has died & fallen.
By a crumbling tree, what was,
weeks ago, a flared sulphur spectacle,
chicken mushroom, unmistakable,
is now a jellied, browning mess, putrid already,
& full of insects whose work is to make
food of decay, as the mushroom did in its turn.
It's such a bustle of transformation, I won't even
prod it with my toe to see what happens.
Somewhere overhead, a cloud shifts, or the wind,
a flickering door opens on the ground ahead,
clearly a shape of light thrown through leaves,
as clearly a way into a place I will never see again.
Each step sinks in leaves layered on each other
like the years of a life—
rich & fertile with decomposition
& the living evidence of the only constant I know
from observation, the way life uses death,
grows up through it, flowers, seeds itself,
& lays itself down in its turn. I had wanted
to taste my first wild mushroom,
but I was too late. Anything might appear in its place.
How could I forget? The dog reads the ground,
snorting & blowing leaf dust—she pulls
to the full length of the leash, pulls me
through the door of light, down avenues
of imminent death & rot. Her wish

42

is to keep moving, following out a scent
& sampling another, each a promise & a history,
each better than the last, too good not to try.

An Adult's Guide to Nightfall

Stitching the dark is restless noise,
clicks & trills, a bass-line pulse, as if
souls released at the death of light thus hum
a way through doubtful night. We thirst,

but lie still in our beds. From shadow
to sight, an opossum bares its Noh-mask face,
a sketch of fear, the tail a cord of flesh
both naked & snake-like. Alien.

Nightly to the woods, by paths that fade,
past gold eyes deep in the trees, we go
like children to find the witch in the clearing.
Sleep is that story we breathe to ourselves

in the uncharted wake of day, a hymn,
from the near bank of light to the far,
of our solo passage, the shape of which
each one must learn, in time, by heart.

Unfiltered

Days of wind-chased rain & now
a first steady chill between gusts. At last,

sunset, peach & gold as a painter's dream
of truth. All at once, it seemed, the light

rose as if it had discovered Earth, saying
in its speechless way, *glory* & *amen.*

It laved the grass & leaves, all still green,
in a gold lie, dyed the clouds & left

the sky such clear & brilliant blue
as to make Technicolor seem no more

than the dim, familiar palette of the real.
We could almost believe the world asks

to be cherished, sometimes, through our fear.
From its great impersonal to our single selves,

down to the cells a part of it, inseparable,
though we stand apart & say a word like *self.*

The dawn of understanding, by induction,
must arrive again as it always has before:

this dusk, trees already-darkened piers
upholding sky, must come & go, give way

to dark, to light, & on (remember)—
out of history, beyond human will.

III. Recitations & Incantations

Weights & Measures

Houses painted on the side of a bridge—
a concrete overpass in Prague, sooted
with exhaust—pastel houses, a bright facade,
the real city dark in the background.
My last sleep from Vienna by train, the car
unheated, the seats royal blue plush.
Three young men offered to carry
my bag & slept politely, hands tucked tight.

Another station, the same cracked platforms,
the same dust in the cuffs, Turkish sludge
in the demitasse, the beer bitter
& warm. Faces indecipherable
in the grayed light of winter. These houses—
have I seen them somewhere? They are pastels

outlined in black, their windows open
but shadowed. Near is a buttressed cathedral,
ropes of rain thread sky through gargoyles' mouths,
silent as the saints around the dimmed
rosette. The walls are scaffold to centuries,
as if what rises inside the great house
could spill over pew & aisle. The pious
kneel & nod their strange prayers, my voice lost

in my throat or a foghorn blaring—its notes
arrange like a code without a key,
the tattoo of rain on cobblestones.
I am not on the map. I am somewhere
I can sense but not say, like a spice which
has no name in my language. In the streets,

unpronounceable, I find the tourists'
Valhalla, where the beer is sweet & cheap,
brown as the wood pews lining the hall.
Everyone's English is broken. We raise
glasses long past midnight. We bring strangers
to strange beds, keep the rooms dark, try forgetting
the sprawling, sooty town, the ghetto,
the castle, the penitent streets. We want

to close our eyes on what we've seen.
An accordion band plays "My Bonnie Lies
Over the Ocean." The clock-tower frames
a wedding, makes a racket that keeps
the world constant. We want the night before
sleep to be filled & the morning, warming

as mulled wine outdoors, the steam sour & sharp.
We wake into glassy silence, the bed
too small, unforgiving——. How darkly forms
are outlined in daylight, how the streets
to town take shape, the great church rising
by the castle again, as we hoped it would.
I pick up words here & there, lose myself
in places where monks float by, recognize

someone I've never met but know well.
Each day is like this. The faces, replaced
as quickly as they go, tell my fortune.
I read their disguises, their halting speech,
their faith in setting out on foot again,
finding the next train, a new, hard bed,

pausing at a few syllables heard
& almost known. Here's what stops me—a feast
of graffiti, houses drawn on an overpass,
a few flat squares that itch of the familiar.
If I could just see through the black windows—
a room I left behind, the table set & waiting,

anger-marks painted over, chairs gone wobbly
under years of weight. Something is happening
there, has happened, will happen, someone will
die unexpectedly, & so, alone—
someone will decide it's time to leave
for good & go—& might be gone already.

Studies in Architecture at the Grocery

It's blinding, but only clean from a healthy distance—
bright tiles, shocking light, canned thunder
emitted by small speakers in the produce aisle
when "rain" is about to mist the declining lettuce.
Ten minutes sorting through the green bell peppers,

looking for the three (for a dollar) that surpass the rest,
each balanced on the arched shoulders of those below,
a delicate structure upset by my diggings—it's clear
that tonight I will not find them, hands too cold
to feel. Here's a tip: no one grocery shops

on Friday night. You have the store to yourself,
or think you do—hence the woman who walked
behind her cart looking at the shelves until
she almost ran me down—hence my lack
of words to warn her. I stared. She looked in time.

We saw we were not alone. Pails of flowers stacked
into pyramids, wires around the stems of Gerber daisies
to help them hold their showy heads up.
All the flowers without names are "wildflowers, $1.39."
They look like terrible imitations of imaginary blooms

in children's books, feel like plastic & that grainy flocking
on some wallpapers or girls' dresses: "dotted swiss."
I could use a wire like the daisies have
to give their soft stems "body," a hint of something
wound around me—not a wick,

but a structural addition, functional & maybe
beautiful like flying buttresses—make me Notre Dame,
hunkering over space, enclosing all those prayers, the kneeling,
the singing, the looking up & turning in, the centuries echoing
inside its stone skin, all that air barely contained in a husk—

a huge cicada shell hooked with something that looks like
    permanence
down by its arching, immovable legs.

One Voice Among Sounds Like an Ocean

In memoriam LPR

Suddenly there is such quiet that someone's voice lifts
startlingly over the busy signal of the crickets,
late summer's last seconds, the springs winding down.
If I stand on the bed to reach two mosquitoes
roosting on the wall where they will roost permanently,

stuck with a smear of my blood, I can hear them
whine away their last bit of time, the sound that comes
always before the little sting.
Ordinarily—by daylight—I wouldn't hear
these moments when the insects stop

as if listening themselves—there is too much
that overlaps, the dump truck's grinding, the jets
taking off & landing, laughtracks & soundtracks,
televisions blinking & speaking from the tops
of pillars in airports like the several mouthpieces of God,

my fellow passengers strapped into planes, trains,
seen in motion through one window or another,
too fast & distracted to meet or touch,
but always talking to someone else, seen or unseen,
at hand, in hand, distant. Such endless conversation,

the quarrels, negotiations, deals. The splitting &
splicing—stitchery & pretending. Conversation
only with the self—revealing enough to require disguise:
a phone, a feigned Other to hear that advice
one wishes someone else would give,

what we tell ourselves & hope it might be wisdom.
The phone a shield, a palmed silence,
a seashell broadcasting waves from any ocean.
A line to your dead boyfriend, held
these long years in a memory that's loosened its ribbons,

thrown to the needy the boxed artifacts only hindsight
would know enough about to wish to keep.
But it is never the restless shade of the lost lover
on the line—*rest, perturbéd spirit!*—; it is a breathy woman
telling me I've won a resort vacation,

or a tired-sounding lady who has dialed correctly,
but without meaning to find, at the end of this connection,
me. It would be nice to think this the sweet voice
from my childhood, but it is not, not someone's grandmother
with an extra blessing for unknown, needful me,

not my own grandmother, who is not dead yet,
although her body—like thought—like sound—
seems not to retain its particular shape anymore.
When I walk into the bedroom before she knows I'm there,
it is almost as though her body has vanished already,

then the face that turns toward mine begins to resemble
the one I remember. The eyes are hers, as direct as ever
in saying she isn't ready, not like this, no one could be ready
for this terribly gradual leaving—I see it & there is now nothing
to say about it.
                    I'm one of those everywhere with a phone

to my ear, saying *it didn't have to be that way, I'm sorry,*
or *how could you leave? come back*—
& the people on either side in the bus, or waiting
near me in the airport with their eyes trained
on the tops of the pillars, looking for good news,

will feel a kind of momentary comfort in thinking I'm trying
to patch it up with someone willing to reconcile & alive.

Imagine the Beast in the Desert

The lion will stalk you long before
you see its golden hide. Too late to run.
Alone, there is no choice. Accept
a last brief look at all this world:

the cat, the watered desert, green, in bloom,
the unfamiliar sky. The unrelenting sun,
an eye fierce & final as a god's,
trained on a sudden stop on an unplanned path.

The sun must read our scribbled lives
through its impartial fire. No. We know
it cannot read, & we have written

nothing by its light. Still, we wish to die
as story or song, a falling & rising
at once, that the end of our line be no end.

How She Left Us

The front row stood & filed past.
Brevity. Ceremony. Prayer. Benediction.
Chairs in rows so we could place ourselves,
loss chained in the channels around nose & mouth,
lilies in wreaths to steady their toppling heads.

The way a man leaving the bedroom
one morning for his lifelong job pauses
by the foot of the bed where his wife is still
turned toward the warmth of shared sleep

& pats her foot, as if to cheer them both
through their separate days until late
when they'll lie together again in the dark,

my grandfather reached out, stooped in the shoulders
after it all, to pat the foot of her casket in passing.

The Sycamore Reminds Me That It, Too, Is Alive

Along the stream, around the bend,
the sycamore gives off light like a god,
dazzles my eyes with its rays—
I swear I can't blink sense into them.

Light blasts all in photons—
the tree grapples earth & sky,
cast inward by the eye, it's torqued colorless,
grayscale, then turned & retouched.

A chemical bath seethes in the lab
of the cortex, the image sunken & drowned—
light's waves & particles excite
belief & longing—

what meets the eye from afar
in the light touches deep
into mineral earth, into bloodied sky,
blazes folded cortex,

flaring along the rhyming branches of neurons,
a forest fire leaping synapses,
casting flocks of shadows in migratory
gusts of meaning

or mourning, the lost acres
of Loth Lorien, Vishnu's mothering
Banyan, a tree holding up the world,
life at the center of life—.

This moment of siren light sings open
a portal light's energy streams through, transformed
in the strange, chemical swamps
of the brain, as real

as anything that matters,
as real as matter, with its branching,
vascular pathways, tree or human
rivered within—what we share is

core, heart, center, wounds bleeding, sap
that drenches the pith of us, feeding our reach,
a rough bark forming to protect
the fontanelle that must be softly touched.

Code Red

The dog startles into barking, howling,
as if he's seen the Four Horsemen.
I walk out softly to look at the world.

On the pine, a nuthatch.
I can see its eye shift, but it doesn't fly.
Nearby, a sparrow on a branch stays immobile.

Has the world stopped after all?

What storm threatens to lash the new
leaves to green lace, what terror is
crumbling the houses?

I hold my breath in the quiet.
The neighbor ambles out to clean the grill.

Time is moving, after all, or doing whatever it can be said to do,
    flowing,
immersing us, holding us to earth,
swirling through the spaces, turning dead leaves to brown lace,
cracking windows, frightening the dog,
who can only see his prey when it's moving.

Anything that keeps still—huddled, tense, silent—is safe.

Desert Bloom

Cactus holding a silk-satin pink-gold bloom
the way you'd say someone holds a torch
for you, trying to set a particular fire,
or light for your flesh a way. *Come to me
with your thirst*, it says,
                        let me feed you
from the green crown cupped at my core, drink
from this, my throat, bared as the mountains
that ring our sky, center of whose circle
we always are. Look how this live bowl has burst
from my side, how here you can touch me
painlessly—see what extravagance I keep
inside my mask of needles, what I offer you
out of diligence, need, a dream of fruit,
before it stitches shut for lack of rain.

Under Cumulonimbus

Noon darkens to charcoal at the edges.
Overhead is lead-dull between spotlights.
The air swaddles us. We walk against wind,
it seems, figures in rough footage, lost
as in a black-&-white past. We move
hardly. What holds us back is
unseen. The words our mouths form,
in silence, might be cries or whispers.
At midday, time is all we believe in,
stretched on a rack of minutes
until the thunderstorm breaks in
to free us. Earth & air build charges,
nothing moves or sings. We breathe.
Darkness, tension, fear, release, & then—

like health after fever, the colors return.
It is difficult to record thought,
even impression—how a summer torrent
whitens the air to opacity—
how the air feels—burdensome—
mornings as we lift ourselves from sleep
—that it is only summer, or winter, or
spring, or fall that makes us dread—
that the cloudburst's violence stalls our counting
—a moment—floods the earth—clears the sky.

Luke Perry, Former Heartthrob, Dead of Stroke at 52

He was no Tom or Tom or Denzel,
not larger than life, but still better.
We now-middle-aged wishful Brendas

longed to soothe his '90s-style-James-Dean
hurt. We named our children Dylan.
It was all we could do

in our real lives. We dreamed he was anything
we wanted him to be, unlike our boyfriends,
husbands, fathers. When he came back

to us as good Fred Andrews, faded father,
forlorn & forthright, furrows careworn
in his brow—like ours, stigmata

of worry & burden—he wore
plaid shirts, jeans, & work boots
Hamlet-like. He *hath*, like us,

that within that passeth show,
the wound unseen. He forgave us
our broken marriages, our wayward,

irreconcilable children. Saint Fred,
patron of goodness under temptation,
of the small-town lost world

that never was any better than rotten
at the core, let our serial dreams
say what they would. Out of the countless

deaths today, this one made us
mourn, this idea's premature grave.
It could have been us. A real man died

too young, & though someone's real loss
will last, we can dream & forget. Thank goodness
for this easy grief, this dress rehearsal.

Still Life with Biopsy

Heat & a ticking of gear teeth, metronome,
music too faint to hear—hand to throat,
she feels it: nothing there before, no hint
of strange silhouette in prescient shadow.
Now a seed splitting hard-hulled to tender,
exceeding itself, floss-fine roots spread

to hold. A marble in cat-eyed dark. A sphere
expands, perimeter points equidistant
from center, but if she could see from there
the borders would be indefinite, star-chart,
planetarium sparkle, the eye seduced:
there the space-station, there, satellites,
natural & man-made. From that center, a model

of this world—world of the hand's holding
the throat—in time-lapse, which means
the camera has seen how it will end.
This world, whose centerpoint, whose axis,
whose molten core also lies under the palm
of her hand ends by exceeding itself with babies,

brushed-chrome appliances, cellophane
wrappers, drivers flipping the bird
from freoned containment. Or it doesn't.
A meteorite craters Arizona again
& we dinosaurs freeze under dust clouds.
Or what? It will be slow—we'll not notice
& we'll be gone. We'll not have heard the ticking,

66

or thought it was meant to soothe,
a cooling engine, lover's tapping finger.
She feels it: breath hung on a brass nail,
mitosis—this no seeded womb but a buried,
pollinated cell, overtime worker who won't
clock out. Not a child growing towards birth,

not here where the poisoned apple stuck,
this trap, this flute she never trusted.
This, a lodger named Grief, rock with crystal
interior, faceted spikes for everything she couldn't say,
compressed to diamond, held there, a stuck pill.
She thought it meant: the flu. Meant: you will cry soon.
Meant: today something big will happen.

A fist of premonition. A drink of soup in her dream
that burned a path down. Waking with tongue raw,
blistered fingertips—it's real. The rib-ringed
tunnel, tendon & muscle strung jaw to clavicle,
flexible column, stem, snapping point
in the wrong hands—easy silk to the knife,

layers peeled back & the gland, maroon cushion
with its stone weight, lifted out to a steel pan,
sliced & malignant evidence. Closing the neck,
a stoma stitched stark black, chromosomes
lined up at center-cell to split. She feels it:
slight depression, thumb-deep. A cup of dark.
Leafed branch shushing & somewhere: storm.

Superfoods: The Cucumber

The name *squash* would suit it, soft-skinned tube
of water and starch. Not exactly sweet,
not quite bitter, almost flavorless,
"a favorite taste of summer," a food
"fit only for cows," a "miracle of health."
Its superpower is to be cool.

In truth, it is always exactly
the same heat as its surroundings.

Its other magic is with wet weight
to draw the bloat & bruise from heavy
eyelids, make them young & sleepless again.

Like any talisman or fetish,
its power relies on belief. Tip
the head back, apply edible disks
to eyes, transform—a seedy, sightless
zombie. Everything's okay, stay cool.
Presto! You look fresh as a salad.
Whatever else you may be, you're alive.

Therefore, slice through the cucumber's skin
or pare it clean off, render its seeded
flesh liquid, drink it, slather its chill pulp
over the thirsty skin of your face—
claim its biochemistry, a life for your life.

Swimming Lessons

I wake as though I've been swimming
all night, rising from cold water to cool air, blue
in the fingertips, almost bruised in the hollows
under my eyes, heading, as I did those summers

at the YMCA, to the shower, steaming
my skin to raise a blush: water to charm away
the chill of water, or take back from sleep what
it has claimed this time. I might as well search

those mornings for the faces of the other
children, the Minnows, the Flying Fish, the Sharks,
& their names, so gone to me now it seems
as though I was alone in the pool. I must've thought so

sometimes, gasping through endless laps of crawl,
the on-off of breaststroke's piston-rhythm:
with each misstroke I'd feel the shameful drag,
from sleek thing slicing along—seal, otter, dolphin—

to bundled carpet, dog or horse churning froth,
no glide, no distance. But, a few laps done, the surface
was sheer silk I ripped with exact fingertips, raising
no splash, each whole arm following through

to the cocked elbow & quick turn for breath, almost
easy—a few more, & it had always been this way,
thrust & glide, the sound of breath expelled in water,
the sound of water opened & closing behind me,

the others splashing, their arms & legs working
at a blue liminal distance, ritual tracings of survival's
story, monotony. How quickly the pool smoothed
when we left: new glass, glimmering, amnesiac.

Graveyard Shift of the Mind

1

Days, I'm like everyone else, my face a coin,
impressed with shapely features, a neat familiar
profile. *The many are one. In God we trust.*
All day, I look up, smile, look away.
I sometimes remember what I haven't said,
whose eyes I didn't meet. The man outside of Walgreen's
asks twice for change—I skirt the space around him,
looking down. My funhouse-mirrored face slides
copperless as new pennies along the skins
of hollow, dentless, shining cars.

2

Low water in the bayou, grocery carts tipped
to sieve it clear: sure traps the mullet escape,
shooting the silvered arrows of their bodies sunward,
anglers on the banks gaping back at them like fish.
Barkless twigs wick sugar up the lengths of knotty trees,
budding into flame, a spectacle
we park-goers take in with wheezing breaths
—our sneakers slap the paths around each other,
strange dancers in a stranger's ballet. False spring,
I can't tell where I end & everything else begins—

3

My rooms fall dark, windows unshaded.
Alone in shadow, I can't be seen but see everything:
night's architecture—black trees filigree the purple-
orange sky, bolstered on black fundamental houses,

& far & bright, the light-studded downtown
gleams like Oz. Only night sleeps anymore—
it dreams the city's incandescence,
its bereft walkers, its sunken-eyed insatiable readers
whose mumbled words people the ancient dark—
night's mendicant, I keep vigil with perpetual freeways,
lie down full & fearless in the first gray light.

Spectacular

I am thinking again of the world
seen magnified through field-glass eyes,
in which a winged blur crossing the field is lost

to focus, found swaddled in light, & lost
again with an arm's tremor, a bird-like
twitch almost in wing-sympathy. My eyes

are slow to find even landmarks—see nothing
at first—then grow sharp, addressing the world-shaped
lenses as though I were the hawk, or

had learned its way: to listen with the eyes or
entire self for heartbeat, movement. I am easily lost
tracking sleek heron-heads across dense worlds

of swamp, quiet & alone. I only want the bird
to be, stalking, working some squirm-thing
down its gullet: one white Great egret turns an eye

in my direction, meeting, perhaps, my doubled eyes
goggling at patterns, green or
brown foliage, scoured blue, steel water, each thing

integral to itself as I am to myself. Lost
in simply sensing, I swear I never thought a bird
could show me how to be in this world

I'm not certain I belong to—as the egret, in the human world,
is misfit, stark wonder. How many "I's"
I've invented, trying to find the one that would glide,

bird-plumed, into grace. I mean naturalness, or
ease, a generosity of being I'd like to think is not lost
forever to me or us, fortified, encircled with things:

phones, cars, screens, these mediating things
bricked up around our lives. They aren't the only world.
What can I do?
                    —Lift the glasses or
scope again, steady my arm, turn the focus sharp: a bird
forms in the field, something spectacular. And I
find myself in this world, not unformed or ugly or lost.

Running

You can't approach it step
by step

or gravity will fell you
like *lumber*—

that verb you think to
punish yourself

when your legs lag
less than *limber,*

dully sullen children gone limp
revolutionaries

of inertia dragging the bedraggled
banner of ennui.

Legs like sodden pasta
or not,
       the key is to stop thinking—

a few hardwon minutes wordless,
wheezing breaths or not,

a plane slicing smooth curls off
the surface of time, evening it out,

silkening as you glide almost frictionless,
almost light, finally nothing

more than alive.

Acknowledgments

Many thanks to the following publications, in which some of these poems first appeared, some in slightly different form or under different titles:

"Until Daylight & the Train," *KAIROS* (Editors' Prize, 2020-21)

"Pyrite & Mica", *Many Mountains Moving*

"Gulf," *The Midnight Oil*

"Retraction," *IthacaLit*

"Consignment," "Still Life with Biopsy," *Phoebe*

"Spectacular," *Ellipsis*

"Studies in Architecture at the Grocery," *New Letters*

"One Voice among Sounds Like an Ocean," *American Literary Review*

"Desert Bloom," *Lake Effect*

"Swimming Lessons," *Southern Poetry Review*

"Graveyard Shift of the Mind," *Tex!*

"An Adult's Guide to Nightfall," *the minnesota review*

"Natural Violence," *Los Angeles Review*

"Into the Woods," *Plainsongs Magazine*

"Unfiltered," *Dovecote*

"Greeting a Neighbor in the First Hour of Light," *Cagibi*

"A Big Easy Sestina," *Midway Journal*

"Memory Is a Body Concealed," *Broad River Review*

"Light Is Not the Only Constant," *Southword 39*

"Refusing to See Saltcedars as Weeds," *Zone 3*

"Railway," *Twyckenham Notes*

"Spectacle," *Twyckenham Notes*

"Badlands & Canyon," *Sheila-Na-Gig*

"Running," *Clarion*

About the Author

Jennifer Brown (she/her) lives with her partner, Bret, and a funny-looking dog named Rowlf in Montpelier, VT, having recently left her home state of North Carolina and the too-hot south behind for good. Once upon a time, she studied writing and literature at the universities of Tennessee in Chattanooga, Maryland in College Park, and Houston, collecting a BA, MFA, and Ph.D along with the immeasurable benefit of spending time among fascinating humans. She has taught creative writing and literature in high schools, colleges, summer programs, and festivals and has held residencies at the Weymouth Center for the Arts and the Vermont Studio Center. Her work has appeared in *Copper Nickel, Orison Anthology, Cimarron Review, Zone 3, Twyckenham Notes*, and *Cincinnati Review*.

Our Mission

BRICK ROAD

POETRY PRESS

The mission of Brick Road Poetry Press is to publish and promote poetry that entertains, amuses, edifies, and surprises a wide audience of appreciative readers. We are not qualified to judge who deserves to be published, so we concentrate on publishing what we enjoy. Our preference is for poetry geared toward dramatizing the human experience in language rich with sensory image and metaphor, recognizing that poetry can be, at one and the same time, both familiar as the perspiration of daily labor and as outrageous as a carnival sideshow.

Available from Brick Road Poetry Press

BRICK ROAD

POETRY PRESS

www.brickroadpoetrypress.com

All These Hungers by Rick Mulkey

Escape Envy by Ace Boggess

My Father Should Die in Winter by Barry Marks

The Return of the Naked Man by Robert Tremmel

Available from Brick Road Poetry Press

BRICK ROAD

POETRY PRESS

www.brickroadpoetrypress.com

Also Available from Brick Road Poetry Press

BRICK ROAD
POETRY PRESS
www.brickroadpoetrypress.com

Dancing on the Rim by Clela Reed

Possible Crocodiles by Barry Marks

Pain Diary by Joseph D. Reich

Otherness by M. Ayodele Heath

Drunken Robins by David Oates

Damnatio Memoriae by Michael Meyerhofer

Lotus Buffet by Rupert Fike

The Melancholy MBA by Richard Donnelly

Two-Star General by Grey Held

Chosen by Toni Thomas

Etch and Blur by Jamie Thomas

Water-Rites by Ann E. Michael

Bad Behavior by Michael Steffen

Tracing the Lines by Susanna Lang

Rising to the Rim by Carol Tyx

Treading Water with God by Veronica Badowski

Rich Man's Son by Ron Self

Just Drive by Robert Cooperman

The Alp at the End of My Street by Gary Leising

About the Prize

BRICK ROAD
POETRY PRESS

The Brick Road Poetry Prize, established in 2010, is awarded annually for the best book-length poetry manuscript. Entries are accepted August 1st through November 1st. The winner receives $1000 and publication. For details on our preferences and the complete submission guidelines, please visit our website at www.brickroadpoetrypress.com.

Winners of the Brick Road Poetry Prize

2019

Return of the Naked Man by Robert Tremmel

2018

Speaking Parts by Beth Ruscio

2017

Touring the Shadow Factory by Gary Stein

2016

Assisted Living by Erin Murphy

2015

Lauren Bacall Shares a Limousine by Susan J. Erickson

2014

Battle Sleep by Shannon Tate Jonas

2013

Household Inventory by Connie Jordan Green

2012

The Alp at the End of My Street by Gary Leising

2011

Bad Behavior by Michael Steffen

2010

Damnatio Memoriae by Michael Meyerhofer

www.ingramcontent.com/pod-product-compliance
Lightning Source LLC
Chambersburg PA
CBHW031144090426
42738CB00008B/1218